A Quaker Astronomer Reflects

Jocelyn Bell Burnell

16
EasyRead Large

Copyright Page from the Original Book

Quakers
AUSTRALIA

Produced by Australia Yearly Meeting of the Religious Society of Friends (Quakers) in Australia Incorporated

Printed by UniPrint, Hobart.

Copies may be downloaded from
www.quakers.org.au
or ordered from sales@quakers.org.au
or sales@ipoz.biz

Front cover: On the surface of Mars, looking back along the wheel tracks of the robotic Rover. [Courtesy NASA]

TABLE OF CONTENTS

THE JAMES BACKHOUSE LECTURES

The lectures were instituted by Australia Yearly Meeting of the Religious Society of Friends (Quakers) on its establishment in 1964.

They are named after James Backhouse who, with his companion, George Washington Walker, visited Australia from 1832 to 1838. They travelled widely, but spent most of their time in Tasmania. It was through their visit that Quaker Meetings were first established in Australia.

Coming to Australia under a concern for the conditions of convicts, the two men had access to people with authority in the young colonies, and with influence in Britain, both in Parliament and in the social reform movement. In meticulous reports and personal letters, they made practical suggestions and urged legislative action on penal reform, on the rum trade, and on land rights and the treatment of Aborigines.

James Backhouse was a general naturalist and a botanist. He made careful observations and published full accounts of what he saw, in addition to encouraging Friends in the colonies and following the deep concern that had brought him to Australia.

Australian Friends hope that this series of Lectures will bring fresh insights into the Truth, and speak to the needs and aspirations of Australian Quakerism. The present lecture was delivered at the University of Canberra in January 2013.

Maxine Cooper
Presiding Clerk
Australia Yearly Meeting

About the author

Jocelyn Bell Burnell is a professional astronomer and a Quaker from Britain Yearly Meeting. In the UK she has been President of the Royal Astronomical Society, President of the Institute of Physics and Clerk of Britain Yearly Meeting, and continues to do a lot of committee work for both communities. She has received many scientific prizes, and is much in demand as a speaker and broadcaster.

1. Introduction

Why this subject?

For almost as long as I can remember Friends have been curious about whether I can reconcile science and religion (my academic colleagues are much less concerned). In part this is simply curiosity; but is there also an element of anxiety in their asking? Are they looking for assurance that there is not a problem? I sense also that my being a scientist has provided an element of reassurance and comfort to the Friend on the Meeting House bench; if Jocelyn can somehow be a Quaker and a scientist then it must be OK, even if the Friend concerned doesn't know, or doesn't want to know, the details!!

Although I do a lot of speaking on diverse topics, and enjoy it, I have not found this topic easy and have not rushed to talk (or write) about it. Part of this has been a sense of inadequacy – I have no training in philosophy, theology or the sociology of science, so circumspection would be in order. Part of this is because the personal theology I have evolved seems rather shocking and I don't want unnecessarily to rock other people's fragile boats of belief. And a large part of it is because I'm not at all sure that I have got there yet; in particular I have tried, but failed, to reconcile what my heart and my head have told me. I have always seen this as work in progress and wanted to leave myself room to evolve it. Being a fairly high-profile Quaker, I judged going public might mean I was forever anchored to what I said and would not be given space to change my thinking. Talking on science and religion, whilst providing a stimulus to think about what I did believe, also to a degree serves to fix it and writing about it would probably fix it even more thoroughly.

However, having left myself room to evolve my theology, to be honest, it has shifted very little in the last 20 years! This is not for want of trying; I seem to have stagnated. Now in the year in which I turn 70, there is less of life ahead of me than there used to be and maybe my thinking is not going to evolve much more, so perhaps this is the time, and the opportunity, to put pen to paper.

I have had plenty of opportunity to think about these issues; why has my theology stagnated? Because I got it right first time? Probably not! More likely because I have not understood enough to perceive challenges to it or because of a communications problem – a failure to understand what others are saying about their beliefs. I have also felt the lack of a peer group, of people who understand each other and can discuss these topics without feeling threatened. On the few occasions when I have had opportunity to interact with such a group or individual I have learnt such a lot.

Canberra

Australia Yearly Meeting meets in Canberra this year (2013) – the 60th anniversary of the first Quaker meeting in Canberra. The first meeting was held at Mount Stromlo – at the Observatory in the home of Royal and Bill Buscombe. The astronomer Bill Buscombe (1918–2003) was brought up in Canada and met his wife Royal when they were both undergraduates at Toronto University. Originally an agnostic, he joined Quakers in Toronto before 1939 and he and Royal were married under the care of Toronto Monthly Meeting in 1942. Bill registered as a conscientious objector during World War II and this was recognised by the Canadian authorities.

After graduating with an astronomy degree in 1940 he spent the rest of the war as a meteorologist, forecasting the Atlantic weather for planes and ships' convoys. He had a few years as an astronomer in the United States of America before coming to Canberra in 1952, the year in which Mount Stromlo Observatory (then known as the Commonwealth Observatory) had suffered a bush fire. He did pioneering work on the spectral classification of southern hemisphere stars; from the spectra of stars astronomers can deduce the temperature and luminosity of the star, its evolutionary stage, its mass and radius and whether it has any chemical peculiarities. He subsequently became known for his compilation of the 'MK Spectral Classification Catalogues' – an invaluable tool for professional astronomers.

He and Royal had eight children, four boys and four girls; five of them were born before they came to Canberra, the rest in Canberra. Bill and Royal returned to the USA in 1968, taking the four youngest with them, and he spent the rest of his life there. He and Royal were founder members of Canberra Meeting and after returning to the USA he was active in Evanston Friends Meeting, Chicago.

He is remembered in Quaker circles in the USA for his spiritual depth and the fervour of his commitment. Australia YM's *this we can say: Australian Quaker life, faith and thought* includes a piece written by Royal Buscombe.[1]

My background

I was brought up a Quaker, initially in Ireland YM, in a Northern Irish meeting that was quite evangelical and tended to take the Bible literally. This meeting was scared of science (because of what it might do to religion, I judge) but this wasn't a large factor in my life as at age 13 I went away to Quaker boarding school in the north of England. Here I met a much more liberal kind of Quakerism which fitted well with

---

1 Paragraph 3.80

the way I was heading, and after that I did not return to Northern Ireland for any significant period.

I have since my teens been drawn to the quiet Quaker worship and I have stayed within Quakerism all my life. As a 'birthright' member I have never had to apply for membership (and as a very shy youngster would not have been able to do that). I have learned what membership means by belonging to a number of meetings up and down the UK (I have counted ten) as well as being a sojourning member of Philadelphia YM for a short but intense period.

Each meeting is different and each meeting has drawn different things out of me and helped me grow in areas where I was lacking. Each meeting has given me jobs to do – a further learning experience. I have also served the Yearly Meeting and its committees and for most of my adult life have had a major (but volunteer) role in Quakerism.

At age 12 I had started doing science at school and discovered I was good at it; it looked as if I would be some sort of scientist. My early bent towards science was reinforced by the Soviet Union! In 1957 they launched the first Sputnik satellite.

Until then the USA and the United Kingdom assumed they were ahead of the Soviets technically, but this showed they weren't and it resulted in a push towards science in the UK; anyone who could do science was encouraged to do so. So for me it became a question of what kind of physics I would do.

Soon I 'discovered' astronomy and decided that if I could I would become an astronomer. A physics bachelor's degree led to a PhD in radio astronomy, followed by a precarious period where I struggled to combine family and career and only just managed to stay in or close to astronomy. I discovered I enjoyed teaching and management roles as well as research, and have held several senior management roles in academia.

Now officially retired, I have a visiting position in astrophysics at the University of Oxford and seem to be busier than ever lecturing to all sorts of audiences, serving on committees, judging prizes and so on.

So my science and my Quakerism have matured alongside each other and have become comfortable bedfellows, in ways I will describe in this volume.

Signs for the road ahead

There are many notable scientists who are also religious (as well as some, perhaps higher profile, who are anti-religion). Each of us has our own way, I suspect, of combining those parts of our lives. It is interesting to observe where each of us finds a balance point. Some seem to take their religious faith as given and fixed, and work their science around that; and some take the science as correct and work their faith around it. I tend towards the latter, as readers will see; I am not into apologetics. So this volume may be a tough read for some people, taking unpalatable directions or reaching difficult conclusions.

The timescales I shall be talking about are 'astronomical' – millions if not billions of years and readers may be tempted to ignore anything which will not affect them or their children or their grandchildren. Yes, the timescales are long, and other things will intervene before some of the events I talk about happen, but the reason for looking at these topics is for what they tell us about God. I suspect our theology is astray because we have not thought enough about what the Universe is telling us about the nature of God.

Quaker tradition rightly holds that what matters is how you lead your life rather than what you profess. I agree, but I also believe it is important to understand what underpins your life, why you lead the life you lead.

I apologise if Friends find my conclusions, or my theology unacceptable. As I said above, I fear some may, but above all I have felt the need to be as intellectually honest as possible and to have integrity. I have tried to address real issues – how what we are learning about the cosmos can be integrated with what we read in the Bible, or with conventional Quaker or Christian belief; how our current scientific understanding relates (or fails to relate) to the religion we find around us.

2. Quakers and Science

What the scientist means by 'a theory'

It might be helpful to describe what a scientist means by a theory and the status that should be accorded it. In everyday language theory can mean hunch or speculation, conjecture or guess, but scientists use the word in a more limited and controlled way.

A scientific theory is a picture or an explanation (sometimes called a model) of what we are studying. It is a human creation to help us understand how something might behave, and to provide a basis for testing that behaviour by experiments or observations to gather evidence. An essential part of a theory is that it makes testable predictions; string theory is not yet really a theory, for example, because it has not yet made any testable predictions. The testing builds up a body of evidence that supports or refutes the theory. The theory must be based on naturally occurring phenomena, so for example, suggesting that God created the Universe is not a testable prediction. Theories should always be held provisionally and be modified or discarded as the results of experiments require. Results should normally be confirmed by at least one other research group working independently before they are believed and cause a theory to be modified or abandoned; this is especially true of controversial or surprising results (e.g. that neutrinos can travel faster than light).

It can be that following confirmation of a surprising result we are without a guiding theory for a while. A plethora of highly creative new theories may be suggested, but usually only a few gain some traction and are taken seriously enough to be tested.

Science is a cumulative activity, with subsequent generations of scientists taking advantage of fresh thinking or of technological improvements in equipment to correct, refine or extend a theory. In this way theories become more accurate and more comprehensive explanations, leading to yet more sophisticated predictions.

Suppose the theory stands, is further tested, and further, and still stands. Is it proven? Is it correct?

Many scientific theories such as the atomic structure of matter, the circulation of the blood, are so well established that no new evidence is likely to alter them significantly – often they are referred to as facts. Further investigation of the theory continues but is usually investigating the 'how' not the 'whether'. While it is possible to prove a theory is wrong, it is not possible to prove that it is complete and is the final word. So theories are held provisionally, in the awareness that someday something may come along which will show it to be wrong or (more likely) incomplete.

Some ideas once accepted are now known to apply within a limited domain. For example, Newton's theories are now known to be incomplete – they are good in an every-day domain, but were tactfully reframed by Einstein who showed they were part of a bigger canvas, with different conditions pertaining at the far edges of the canvas.

Good theories are strong, firmly grounded empirically, long lived, and are widely used by scientists. They serve as wonderful tools and are the best insight that we have into the nature of the Universe. They may or may not be correct in an ultimate, absolute sense – but we cannot judge that. Theories also are products of human creativity and tell us something about that, and they often have a strong aesthetic appeal to scientists. Devising and testing theories is how the astronomer engages with the Universe.

It can seem that there is a negative ambience to science (scientists are always disagreeing with each other) because that is the way modern, western science works. Theories are tested to see if they fail, and usually tested until they fail. If it is not recognised that that is normal scientific procedure, then it can appear that science is in disarray, and sometimes there are attempts to discredit uncomfortable scientific results by suggesting that because scientists cannot agree they don't know what they are doing.

Just because theories are provisional we should not denigrate them, imply they are defective and to be dismissed. They are valuable tools, indeed the only intellectual tools we have. When lecturing to a school group I was once heckled by a student who said our understanding of the origin of the Universe was 'only a theory'. I think he was using the word in the non-scientific sense. Some religious groups will use such an argument to counter sound scientific understanding and promote creationism. Our understanding of the origin of the Universe is one of the best established theories we have in astrophysics; it has been in use for about 50 years and has seen off several contenders. It has been tweaked in that time, but its basic premise has not been substantially altered.

Even though I would not expect readers of this volume to be creationists, nonetheless they may find the account I give of the origin of our universe has uncomfortable consequences. I hope they will not succumb in the face of such discomfort to the temptation of thinking that it is only a theory, that maybe there'll be another one along shortly and that they do not need to engage with this. I hope they can face a disturbing picture as I have had to face it.

Evolving and growing understanding

Evolving one's beliefs in the light of experience, as I emphasised in the last chapter, is one of the strengths of Quakerism. It also means there are close parallels between being a research scientist and being a Quaker.

Take time to learn about other people's experiences of the Light ... Appreciate that doubt and questioning can also lead to spiritual growth ...

Spiritual learning continues throughout life, and often in unexpected ways ... Are you open to new light, from whatever source it may come?[2]

Quakerism is a non-dogmatic and non-creedal denomination, with emphasis placed on how we experience the spirit working in our lives and on how we lead our lives. As we grow in maturity it is likely that our experience of the spirit, our understanding of God and therefore also our beliefs will change. Moving on in our beliefs and understanding is not seen as a sign of weakness but is regarded a proper part of being an actively faithful person.

Research scientists also are used to evolving their picture (or model) of whatever it is they are studying as they do experiments and acquire more data. Indeed the whole purpose of an experiment is to check out their picture and so they live on the edge, at the frontier of knowledge. Their picture may be right and the experiment confirms it, but even then subsequent experiments may show deficiencies in the picture. More likely the experiment shows that the starting picture was inadequate and requires modification.

Sometimes scientists becomes too attached to their picture and are unwilling to accept it needs modification, but mostly we are prepared to move on, and indeed enjoy the chase, the ever shifting scene; we hold our pictures provisionally. The data carry a lot

---

2 Parts of Advices and Queries numbers 5 and 7, Britain Yearly Meeting

of authority – they determine whether the picture is right; this is a point I will return to shortly. Furthermore a good research scientist will be willing to say 'I don't know' or 'We don't know' if asked a question on a topic that has not yet been thoroughly researched. It would be considered bad practice to do otherwise.

Authority in science and authority in (liberal) Quakerism

One aspect of Quakerism that is not always appreciated is how unusual we (and I speak here of liberal, unprogrammed Friends) are in what we consider authoritative. Any church, denomination, world faith can get its authority from its holy writings (the Bible, the Koran etc), from its history (including what its founder said) or from what is called continuing revelation – God speaking to us today. These things are the points of reference for the faithful when the world presents them with a dilemma – that is what I mean by authority. Different faith bodies will put different emphases, giving different weights to these three. For example, the Christian denominations that I have interacted with in ecumenical work usually give an important place to the Bible. Liberal Friends are very unusual in that we give relatively little weight to the first two and place a lot of weight on what we feel God is calling us to do today – we are open to leadings and promptings.

Of course this has pitfalls and we have had to develop checks and balances in order not to be led astray by the articulate but misguided. We have developed practices that involve a meeting corporately considering and weighing what an individual Friend feels led to do and only if the meeting feels that is a right leading can the individual Friend involved go ahead in the name of the Religious Society of Friends. So there is community moderation.

Authority in science is usually assumed to lie with experimental data; if an experiment shows that a theory is wrong, it is wrong (at least in that aspect). However I argue that this is too simplistic and it ignores the role of one's peer group or scientific community. Who decides if a theory has been tested enough and it is time to assume it is broadly correct? It is a consensus decision by the community that it would be a waste of time to further test that theory.

Furthermore it is one's peer group that decides whether one's work gets published, or funded, whether one gets a job or an award; judgement is involved. And where judgement or discernment are involved subjective issues can become relevant; there can be fashions, and bandwagons coming into play, preconceptions and background matter. Those that do not conform to group norms may suffer.

Scientists are not always good at recognising that they are not as objective as they think they are, that they bring cultural baggage. A lot of science is done in community and community matters; here too there is community moderation.

Other science-religion issues

Each summer I give a lecture at the University of Bath as part of a course for overseas students who need to improve their English before entering a UK university in the autumn to start a degree course. They come from all disciplines: arts, humanities, science, business, engineering.

Many years I talk about where some of the chemical elements found in our bodies, such as oxygen, carbon, calcium and iron, come from (answer – the stars). It involves talking about our best understanding of how the Universe began, and at the end of the talk I am frequently approached by (male) Islamic students, newly arrived in Europe, who are keen to convince me that the Koran speaks clearly of these matters. Several have sent me abridged versions of the Koran or other literature demonstrating the Koran anticipated modern cosmology. This is not peculiar to Islam – on the Web one can find the equivalent Christian material showing the Bible predicted (and indeed predated) modern cosmological discoveries.

I note several things from these encounters. First, an obvious weakness in all these arguments is that they are post hoc – if the 'predictions' had been made in advance of the astronomical discoveries they would carry much more weight. I note that sometimes there can be an underlying religious agenda to prove that the scriptures are all-knowing; indeed some people are made quite anxious by the thought that there may be phenomena in the Universe that are unexplained in their religious texts.

A further observation is that it is sad if students come to university so anxious to defend what they have previously learnt that they cannot even engage with new ideas; I hope that these students relax as they get used to being in the UK and allow themselves to at least consider other ideas.

And the final point is to note the danger of rewriting things through the prism of one's own faith; whether I have avoided this I leave to the reader to judge! There is a fine line to be drawn; as Quakers we are encouraged to speak from our own experience, but equally we should avoid characterising the world prematurely using just our own tinted glasses.

Girls' boarding schools in the UK sometimes have had difficulty getting good science teachers. One year our school chemistry teacher, when asked why copper and sulphur and oxygen combine the way they do to make copper sulphate told us 'God made it so'! I later discovered he could have told us about the periodic table and electron orbitals.

This is an example of the sort of piety I can do without. It ignores mainstream, rational scientific explanation and replaces it with a mystery, which apparently only those in league with the devil would wish to question. Such attitudes do little for either science or religion. There may well be dimensions of God that are unknowable, and indeed there are frequent occasions in both science and religion where I have to say 'I don't know' – but this was just a case of ignorance or intellectual laziness.

As a teenager I looked for proof of the existence of God, but quickly came to realise that I was not going to find anything concrete or conclusive. I judged that our world and our God did not go in for black and white unassailable proofs; that our whole existence was more subtle, more diverse, more various than I had at first suspected, and more open. And rather than being a given, fixed entity, set in stone forever, the world was dynamic and I was an organic part of it.

If there was a proof of the existence of God, a lot of effort and attention would go into checking that out, scrutinising it, attacking it. Our faith is all the stronger for having to live in a mature way with the un-provable.

Anthropic principle

This confusing and confused term covers several similar but distinct ideas. It starts from the observation that our (human) existence requires that each of about half a dozen fundamental physical constants lies within a narrow range. For example, if the Universe were a lot younger the stars would have produced less carbon, so life would not be possible; if it were a lot older then stars like the Sun would be dying and there would not be a star to provide us with energy. Or if gravity were a lot stronger we might have a universe of black holes and nothing else. Or if the expansion of the Universe were faster there might not be a solar system of planets.

Although we have not seen any evidence for quantities like the speed of light or the strength of gravity being different in other parts of the observable Universe, we should remind ourselves that we live in an evolving universe and strictly speaking are talking about the value of these constants now (give or take a few million years).

There are various ways to 'explain' this feature of the fundamental physical constants: *a*) the Universe just happens to be the way it is; *b*) there is an, as yet undiscovered, Theory of Everything which requires the Universe to have these values for the physical constants; *c*) there is some, as yet undiscovered, principle which makes the Universe evolve towards life and consciousness; *d*) it is due to intelligent design – it is designed by a Creator God to be that way; *e*) actually none of this is real – we are all part of some higher civilisation's computer simulation; *f*) we are part of a multiverse (more of that in a moment).

Note that many of these (highly creative) 'explanations' are untestable.

The multiverse concept arises naturally from string theory and has been studied for a number of years. Think of bubbles in Edam cheese, or bubbles in a foam (perhaps of dish-washing liquid). Each bubble is a separate universe, and in each bubble these crucial physical parameters can take different values. Some universes (with values in the right range) will allow the evolution of life and some will not. We live in one of those which does.

So far it has not been possible to test any of these ideas, so we do not know if they are correct, but they are attractive!

The Universe does appear to be fine-tuned to our needs, so it is reasonable to ask if this is coincidence, or does it imply intelligent design. How we respond can be very revealing – we often show what we would like to be true. However, there is a danger here, I believe, of putting the cart before the horse: life has been fine-tuned by evolution to fit where we are; if the Universe were very different we would not be here (at least in this form); we, as we are, could only be in a universe like this or very close to this. Our 'good fit' does not prove the existence of intelligent design or a Creator God.

I will end this section by noting that there is an experimental test we might be able to do one day which could throw some light on the question, although would not constitute a proof. Firstly, for each of the crucial physical constants we determine the range that would allow life; e.g. how strong or how weak could gravity be and we still have a universe where life could exist. Having determined the 'allowable ranges' for all the physical constants we then see where the actual values found in our universe fall within these allowable ranges. If they all fall right in the centre of their allowable range I would suspect a creator. If they are randomly scattered within their ranges, with some at the low end, some at the high end, some towards the centre, it sounds more like we are one of a multiverse and we just happen to have this set of constants – it's the luck of the draw or the way the dice fell.

3. Stars, planets and moons

This chapter describes our current understanding of how stars evolve, what we have learnt about the origins of our Solar System, and what we are learning about planets around other stars. But first a quick reminder – planets go round stars and moons go round planets! Putting them in alphabetic order (moons, planets, stars) is also putting them in order of increasing size. Stars, like our sun, shine, generating their own energy. Planets shine, but that is because they reflect light from 'their' star, their sun – they do not produce their own light. And moons also shine by reflecting light from their sun.

The night sky, on a clear night from a dark site is an awesome sight – black velvet studded with diamonds! We can see several thousand stars with the naked eye and we can see some clusters of stars (typically some globular clusters). With binoculars or telescopes we see even more. Before we had street lights, security lights and pollution humans were much more familiar with the dark and the night sky, understood the seasons and the rising and setting of the stars, knew the phases of the Moon and the movements of the planets.

We may have lost much of that, but our understanding of the Universe has been expanded. In the last hundred years we have recognised that many of the nebulae we could see were actually external galaxies, each containing thousands of millions of stars, and so have come to appreciate the scale of the Universe. Bigger telescopes, which can see fainter objects further away in space and earlier in time, have been built. New branches of astronomy such as radio, infrared and X-ray astronomy (most of which stem from technological developments in World War II) have opened our eyes to invisible material like gas and dust, stars in the process of formation and black holes. We have come to appreciate that things in the Universe evolve, that they are not stable for ever, and we have learnt that our universe itself is not stable but also evolves. The pace of change in astronomy itself has accelerated in the last fifty years with new results rolling in and theories having to be revised if not completely scrapped. It has been an exciting time to be an astrophysicist!

Evolution of the stars

Our Sun is a star; it looks different because it is much closer than any other star, but we understand it to be a fairly typical star in many respects, a common kind of star. Like all stars it was born, it has a limited lifetime and it will ultimately die. It was formed about five billion[3] years ago and is now in a long, fairly stable phase; it will likely live for another

---

[3] I am using the USA rather than the UK convention here – a billion is a thousand million.

five billion years – it is about halfway through its life. It shines because of nuclear fusion reactions taking place in its core, converting hydrogen to helium and releasing some energy which emerges as light. It is consuming 600 million tons of hydrogen every second. Although formed five billion years ago, compared with most stars, it is recently formed, a johnny-come-lately. I will return to this point at the end of this section.

Stars form in some of the dark parts of a galaxy; these dark parts are clouds of dust and gas molecules and usually are sufficiently dense (averaging about a thousand particles in a thimble full) that light is absorbed. The Coalsack is an example of such a cloud in our galaxy. The lack of light allows the existence of molecules that would have been broken up in a brighter place, and the study of these molecules and their parent clouds is a new rich field of study. We have found molecules of water, of wood and grain alcohol, of carbon monoxide and of ammonia, and up to a hundred other molecules, in these clouds, and given how very tenuous are the clouds, it is surprising that any chemistry can occur to create these molecules!

Star formation starts when some parts of a cloud collapse in on themselves; the knots so formed have slightly higher gravity and pull in some more of the surrounding material. This puts up the gravity and so yet more material is pulled in. Gradually over a period of perhaps a million years the temperature in the

Figure 1. Ancient white dwarf stars. They shine because they are still hot, but as they shine they cool. The X-shaped spikes are produced in the telescope and are not part of the stars. [Courtesy NASA]

centre of each knot rises and when it reaches about ten million degrees Kelvin nuclear fusion reactions start. It is now a star that shines.

The vast majority of the stars that we can see are, like the Sun, generating light through the nuclear fusion of hydrogen to helium. However, what happens next when the hydrogen in the core of the star runs out, depends on how massive the star is. The large majority of stars, including the Sun, have a short phase with another nuclear fusion reaction (converting helium to carbon); in this phase the star swells and cools, becoming reddish in colour – a 'red giant', like Aldebaran in the Hyades. So in about five billion years from now the Sun will swell a hundred fold in size, will engulf the planets Mercury and Venus and will come close to, if not actually, engulfing Earth. Earth will be uninhabitable. (Actually planet Earth will probably become uninhabitable sooner than that; as the Sun goes through its ten billion year long, 'hydrogen burning' phase its temperature very gradually rises. In about a billion years from now it will be high enough to boil the oceans on Earth. As we approach that point Earth will become uninhabitable.)

After the red giant phase the Sun ceases to generate energy (as will stars like it). It will shrink in size (a matchbox full would weigh a ton) but will still be hot, so becoming what is called a 'white dwarf'. These stars gradually cool, changing from white-hot to yellow, to orange, to red and brown and finally black (invisible). Sirius' companion star, Sirius B, is a white dwarf.

Stars more massive than the Sun, for example the stars in the Pleiades, which are ten to 30 times the mass of the Sun, have a more exciting existence. In their prime they are very luminous stars; because they are more massive their central temperatures are higher and the nuclear reactions go faster generating more light. Even though they are more massive than the Sun they are running at a so much a faster a rate that their lifetime is much shorter.

So the stars in the Pleiades are bright and young – less than about 100 million years old (young by astronomical standards!) and will die young, in something like 30 million years. They have a more exciting end than the Sun, too, and are of prime importance for our existence. A massive star, like one of the bright stars in the Pleiades exhausts the hydrogen in its core after about 70 million years and converts all its available helium to carbon, in half a million years. Over the next 600 years it converts carbon to elements like neon, sodium and magnesium then in six months converts oxygen to silicon and in its final day converts silicon to sulphur, argon, calcium, then iron and nickel ... and then explodes! The explosion, called a supernova is, catastrophic – 95 per cent of the star's material is thrown out into space. Betelgeuse in Orion is a large star that will explode like this one day (but not soon by our timescales, and it is not close enough to cause us any problems when it does explode).

In our bodies there is calcium (in our bones), oxygen (in our lungs), carbon (in our tissues) and iron (in our bloodstream). The atoms of carbon, oxygen, calcium and iron in our bodies were forged inside big stars like those in the Pleiades and made available through the death-explosion of the star. We are indeed made of star stuff, there is stardust in our veins, and if it were not for the life, and particularly the explosive death, of these large stars we would not exist. The material from the exploded star, enriched in elements like calcium, iron, fans out through space, some of it finding its way into the dark molecular clouds where new stars are forming, and so the new stars are enriched in these elements. If some of these new stars are massive ones, they will generate yet more carbon, iron ... and at the end of their lives will explode, distributing their doubly enriched gas across space.

Our Sun is a third generation star – the material it is made from has typically been through two of these explosive stellar cycles, and those exploding stars could have been anywhere in our galaxy. This planet and all that is on the Earth have been formed from the same material as the Sun. So we are made of star stuff, or less romantically, the debris from some stellar nuclear reactions!

The early Universe provided only hydrogen and helium (more about that later) and so could not have sustained life. To provide the diversity of chemical elements needed for life to evolve we had to wait for two generations of massive, exploding stars to do their thing and create enough of the other chemical elements. That is why we are on a planet of a star that is more recently formed than many stars, and why our Sun is a late arrival on the stellar scene.

It always pays to watch the bottom line! The bottom line here is that this great diversity of chemical elements is being created at the expense of hydrogen

– the hydrogen in the Universe is being used up ... and hydrogen is what new stars need to light up.

Planets

Our Sun is accompanied by eight planets which were formed at the same time as it; Pluto was captured later. While we expect to find a lot more dwarf planets like Pluto out beyond Neptune as our telescopes get better, we do not expect to find more regular planets. Of the planets, Earth is at just the right distance from the Sun to support life – not too cold and not too hot; it lies within what astro-biologists call the 'habitable zone' – the band around the Sun where water would be in liquid form.

One of the surprising discoveries in the last ten years has been that lots of other stars have planets! The number is growing rapidly at the moment; at the time of writing (August 2012) a total of 777 such 'exoplanets' are known, and there are a further 2321 candidate planets orbiting 1790 host stars awaiting confirmation. The known planets orbit stars that are broadly the same age as our Sun and have similar amounts of the elements heavier than helium. However, it appears these other planetary systems can be very different from our Solar System.

Our search techniques are still evolving and so we do not yet have a representative sample – for example the two most successful techniques (so far) more readily find planets close to the star and may not pick up ones further out. So at the moment we do not know of many planets that lie in their parent star's habitable zone, but it would be wrong to assume at this stage that they are rare. However, when we look at the night sky and see the stars it is appropriate to reflect that there are probably as many planets up there as the number of stars we can see. I commend the 'Kepler Orrery'* to readers interested in this new field; this animation shows the orbits of many of the known planets around their host stars.

[* http://kepler.nasa.gov/multimedia/animations. Accessed 1 August 2012.]

Could we detect life on an exoplanet? It is possible (but not easy) to study the atmosphere of an exoplanet where there could be several signatures of life. For example, biological activity on the surface of a planet usually drives its atmosphere out of chemical equilibrium, so biological activity could be detected. Of course, this does not necessarily mean that there is intelligent life there.

Moons (natural satellites)

Even in our own Solar System there is great variety in the number and size of moons around the planets. Following the successful Cassini satellite mission we now know Saturn has at least 62 moons as well as the spectacular system of rings.

Figure 2. On the surface of Mars, looking back along the wheel tracks of the robotic Rover. Note the shadow of the Rover at the bottom right. NASA has recently placed another Rover called Curiosity on Mars. [Courtesy NASA]

The gravitational effects of its existing moons produce the banding in the rings and prevent the rings from being formed into further moons. Our early Solar System had a disk of material around the young Sun like a giant version of the rings round Saturn. The material in the rings gradually merged to make the larger planets (and in this case the gravitational effects of the existing planets, especially Jupiter, prevented the material in the Asteroid Belt from forming another planet).

Earth's Moon was formed in the early days of the Solar System, during what astronomers call the heavy bombardment phase, when there were still frequent collisions between recently formed planets and other large lumps of material. One of these large lumps (about the size of Mars) collided with the young Earth and a large piece of the Earth's mantle was flung off, forming the Moon.

Figure 3. Saturn's rings and moon Enceladus [Courtesy NASA]

4. Galaxies and the Universe

This chapter describes our current understanding of galaxies and of the Universe, and how the Universe as a whole evolves, or at least, those parts of the story that are relevant here. It is not meant to be a complete account of the history of the Universe.

The Sun is one of about 100 thousand million stars that form our galaxy, the Milky Way. The Milky Way looks like a faint milky band across the sky (most individual stars are too faint too see), hence the name, but some traditions and myths have given it other names – an Australian Aboriginal name is 'The Rainbow Serpent'. From a dark spot (outside a city) we do not need a telescope or binoculars to see the Milky Way itself, that whitish band of stars, and in the southern hemisphere we can even see two small nearby (but distinct) galaxies, the Large and Small Magellanic Clouds.

The Milky Way is a typical 'spiral galaxy'; it is a thin disk shape (like a flat plate), about 100 thousand light years[4] across. In addition to the stars there are dark clouds of dust and gas (where stars form) and, when a spiral galaxy is seen face on, the stars and dust trace out loosely coiled lanes called spiral arms.

---

4   A light year, the distance light travels in a year, is approximately 10 million million kilometres (or 6 million million miles).

The Sun, the Earth and the other planets are located about two thirds of the way out from the centre of the Galaxy, in one of the spiral arms.

Our Galaxy looks a little like the firework called a Catherine Wheel or a pin wheel, and it spins like one. The rotation of the Galaxy is such that we are moving in the direction of the northern hemisphere constellation Cygnus at 220 kilometres per second (approximately 800 thousand kilometres per hour). Since the formation of the Solar System we have gone about 15 times round the Galaxy. Incidentally as we orbit the Sun each year we travel at 30 kilometres per second or about 100 thousand kilometres per hour and as the Earth spins daily on its axis, at latitudes like Canberra's we are whirling round at about 220 kilometres per hour.

We do not see our Galaxy in the same way as we see other external galaxies because we live inside this plate or pinwheel shape. When we look out we may be looking through the thinnest part of the surrounding 'plate', in which case we see relatively few stars. Or we may be looking in a direction that is through most of the material of the 'plate', and in these directions we see many stars. Whenever we look towards the rim of the 'plate' we will see the most stars, so there is this band around us where the stars are thickest, the Milky Way.

The high speed of rotation of galaxies has turned out to be a problem. Looking carefully at a galaxy we can estimate how many stars and how much dust and

Figure 4. Part of the Pinwheel Galaxy M101 showing the central
hub and spiral arms of stars and the darker dust clouds
[Courtesy NASA]

gas there is in it; so we can get an estimate of its
total mass and therefore estimate how strong is its
gravity. It turns out that typical galaxies are spinning
so fast that they should fly apart – that there is not
enough gravity in the galaxy to hold it together
given how fast it spins. We have many photos of
galaxies and while we quite often see examples of
galaxies merging we see no sign of galaxies breaking
up as they spin. We have been forced to conclude
that there must be extra material in a galaxy which
provides gravity (and helps hold it together) but
does not shine (so we cannot see it). We have
named this material 'dark matter'. I'll say more

about dark matter in the section on clusters of galaxies.

How many galaxies are there in the Universe? A famous British Quaker astrophysicist, Arthur Stanley Eddington, drew up a multiplication table for the Universe. We now know that some of the lines in his table were wrong, but the following two lines are still pretty good estimates:

> *One hundred thousand million stars equals one galaxy,*
> *One hundred thousand million galaxies equals one universe.*

A galaxy is surprisingly empty; as an analogy imagine the largest building you know – perhaps a cathedral or an exhibition hall – with all the furniture removed. Now imagine putting into that empty building a few grains of sand; that is how densely packed is a galaxy! Most galaxies have a massive black hole at their centre and the Milky Way is no exception; however our black hole is smaller than average at a mere four million times the mass of the Sun. Galaxies have been built up by the merger of smaller galaxies (their black holes and all). We can see evidence of several smaller galaxies having merged with the Milky Way. There are rarely direct hits during a merger but gravitational tides can cause great trails of gas and stars to be flung out of the merging hubs.

Figure 5. A pair of interacting galaxies (Arp 273); the galaxies are probably in the process of merging and tidal interactions have pulled out great trails of material. The stars are in the foreground (i.e. in our own Galaxy). [Courtesy NASA]

Clusters of galaxies and superclusters

To complete the picture I will mention that galaxies, themselves groupings of stars, also tend to cluster, with between 100 and several thousand galaxies in a cluster. The Milky Way belongs to a cluster, uninspiringly called The Local Group. The Large and Small Magellanic Clouds are part of the Local Group, as is the Andromeda Galaxy. Clusters of galaxies also tend to cluster into superclusters, but there the hierarchy seems to end. Our supercluster is called the Virgo Supercluster.

Figure 6. Part of the Coma cluster of galaxies; all the 'blobs' and many of the small spots in this photo are galaxies, each of hundreds of thousands of millions of stars. [Courtesy NASA]

The galaxies in a cluster mill around randomly, but seem to be held in the cluster – like people moving around at an open-air reception or drinks party. The curious thing is that individual galaxies seem to be moving so fast they should escape from the combined gravity of the other galaxies making up the cluster. Just as we saw with the speed of rotation of individual galaxies which ought to cause them to fly apart, here too clusters should 'evaporate' as the faster moving galaxies are no longer held and escape from the clusters. We see little evidence of this actually happening, so here again we have had to invoke the 'dark matter' to provide additional gravity to hold on to the rapidly moving galaxies.

There are two disturbing things that we do know about dark matter. The first is the amount of dark matter required – of all matter[5] the dark matter makes up about 85 per cent, the other 15 per cent being the stuff we are (reasonably) familiar with. The second disturbing thing is that while we still do not know what dark matter is, we do know it cannot be made of protons, neutron and electrons – it has to be totally different from the 15 per cent of matter we are familiar with.

Seeing back in time

Light waves and radio waves travel very fast, but not infinitely fast. If you have ever used satellite phones you will be familiar with this – there can be an appreciable delay while your sentence travels up to the satellite and down to the person you are speaking to, and then similarly for their reply to get back to you.

Light and radio waves travel about a foot in a nanosecond or 300 million metres per second. When studying the Universe we need to allow for the time it has taken light to reach us from distant objects.

---

5   Note that at this point I am talking about matter alone, not matter-energy, which we will get to later.

Light takes eight minutes to reach us from the Sun, four years from the next nearest stars, some 30 thousand years from the centre of our Galaxy, 170 thousand years from the Large Magellanic Cloud and millions or billions of years from the more distant galaxies in the Universe. So if tonight we look at the Large Magellanic Cloud (LMC), for example, the light which our eyes pick up from it set off on its journey to Earth 170 thousand years ago; we see the LMC as it was when that light set off all that time ago. If the LMC were (for some inexplicable reason) to stop shining tonight it would be 170 thousand years before we on Earth knew. The deeper into space we look the greater is this time lag, and the further back in time we are seeing.

Birth, life and death of the Universe

The material in this Section is a summary of our current best understanding of the history and evolution of the Universe. Like everything else in science it is open to revision, but the main element of the theory has been around for 50 years, has withstood many tests which rival theories have failed, and its main themes are widely accepted. There are some newer addenda to that theory (particularly dark matter and dark energy), and I will make clear where we are dealing with more tentative material. I will focus on those parts of the theory relevant to the birth and death of the Universe and will not attempt to give a complete account of all aspects of cosmology. For those who wish to learn more there are suggestions for further reading in the Appendix.

There is a hymn which describes the stars as unchanging; that is wishful thinking! Just as we have learnt that the stars are born, live and die, albeit with a lifespan long compared with that of human beings, so it appears that our universe had a beginning and will, on an even longer timescale, have an end.

The Big Bang (its official name) marked the start of our universe 13.7 billion years ago. It seems that all of space, and all of matter and energy were in a very small volume (smaller than a grain of sand) which 'exploded'. What the scientist calls time started with that explosion. These two sentences need some unpacking (and even then they hurt the head)! I envisage all of space folded up inside that tiny volume as like a leaf bud before it opens – all the leaf and its potential for growth are inside the bud. So all of space and its potential for expansion are inside that small volume. When the leaf bud bursts the leaf unfurls and grows (expands). Similarly I picture the early universe unfurling, stretching out and expanding.

A consequence of all of space being tightly crinkled up inside that tiny volume is that all of space was involved in the expansion. The expansion was 'everywhere', or put differently, there was no central spot from which it expanded. Also it is not possible for the scientist to say what came before the Big

Bang, or how that tiny volume containing everything came to be there. Time started with the Big Bang – before the start has no scientific meaning.

Initially the Universe was a giant fireball, but as it expanded it cooled and the radiation energy started to be converted to sub-nuclear particles. After a few minutes it had cooled sufficiently that recognisable particles were formed – the nuclei of hydrogen and helium atoms. It continued expanding and cooling and the formation of the nuclei of the other, heavier elements in any quantity was not possible – particles were too spread out and with too few encounters to make other nuclei. As explained above, for the subsequent creation of the other chemical elements, we needed the stars. Stars and galaxies formed some hundreds of thousands of years after the Big Bang.

One of the pieces of evidence for the Big Bang is that, because of the stretching out of space, we can still see the galaxies moving apart – the expansion of the Universe continues today. Indeed if we could make a film of today's expansion and run it backwards we would see that there was a time when all the galaxies were together in the same place. Another piece of evidence for the Big Bang is that we can still see some of the radiation from the fireball. The expansion of the Universe has spread it out thinly and cooled it to a few degrees above absolute zero; it now is found in the microwave part of the spectrum and is known as the Cosmic Microwave

Background. We discovered it in the 1960s and it has become a major source of information about the early Universe.

There is a third piece of evidence which I will state but will not attempt to explain in detail. It concerns the element deuterium (heavy hydrogen). Stars do not alter the amount of deuterium in the Universe, so the amount we see is the amount produced in the Big Bang. It turns out that different theories about the early Universe predict very different amounts of deuterium and the amount we see fits very well with the hot Big Bang theory.

About 15 years ago we realised that this was not the whole story – and astronomers in Australia (indeed Canberra) were major participants in this development. We had expected that because of the gravity between clusters and superclusters of galaxies that the expansion of the Universe would gradually slow. Evidence accumulated however that the expansion was getting faster; not only were the galaxies, clusters etc. moving apart, but that they were moving apart faster and faster – counter to all reasonable assumptions the expansion was being accelerated! There are today several independent lines of evidence that suggest this phenomenon is indeed true..

We have called whatever is causing this acceleration 'dark energy' (not to be confused with dark matter introduced earlier). At the time of writing we are very unclear what exactly this is. It can be seen in the most recent half of the Universe's history.

Whether it was there before and was simply masked by stronger effects or (less likely) it has only come into being in the last seven billion years we do not know. There are theories which predict that dark energy will decrease with time and theories which predict it will increase! A lot of astronomer-brainpower is now directed to research about dark energy and clearly we are only at the beginning of this particular road.

We have known for some time that energy can convert into matter (as it did soon after the Big Bang) and conversely, matter can convert into energy, so rather than talk about matter or energy separately we tend to talk about matter-energy. Einstein's famous equation, $E=mc2$, shows how much energy can be converted into how much matter and vice versa. Rather startlingly it appears that dark energy accounts for approximately 72 per cent of the matter-energy in the Universe – it is a huge component of our universe.

The presence of large amounts of dark matter and dark energy has affected how our universe has evolved. Today our universe looks like a giant version of stretched out candy floss – filaments, wisps and threads making networks with space (voids) between. The filaments are made of clusters and superclusters of galaxies plus their accompanying dark matter. So when we probe deep into space we can see that the galaxies and clusters of galaxies are not uniformly spread through space but do gather in these lanes.

We also believe that the Universe is flat – it has no curvature and is probably infinite; however because of the finite age of the Universe we can only observe a finite volume of it (out to about 40 billion light years).

Living in an expanding universe means that there may be distant parts of it which appear to be moving faster than the speed of light relative to us, and as a consequence are invisible to us. Living in a universe where the expansion is accelerating means that with time more and more of the Universe will become invisible to us. Our skies will become emptier until our Galaxy appears to be alone in the Universe. If the acceleration is very strong our Galaxy itself could be disbanded; however it is not clear that the acceleration is that strong.

One thing that will happen in the distant future is that the stars will go out. Remember the 'bottom line' from the previous chapter? All those useful chemical elements like oxygen, carbon, gold are formed inside stars, and at the expense of hydrogen. There will come a time when in some dark clouds new stars will form, but will not light up because they do not contain enough hydrogen to start shining. Meanwhile the old stars will be reaching the ends of their lives and fading. So there will come a time when the old stars die and no new stars start – the lights will go out. Black holes will continue to prosper attracting into themselves anything that comes too close, but nothing else will show any sign of life.

5. Implications of this science for beliefs

In discussing the implications of all this astronomy and cosmology for our beliefs I need to stress again that I am taking a very long view. The implications are more for our theology, for how we picture God and God's interaction with us on Earth, than for how we now living on Earth lead our lives – except that our theology in a subtle way shapes our lives.

A friend gets upset when I talk about space, its size, its age and how it is cold, dark and empty; it depresses him, makes him feel small, he says. And others have expressed similar anxieties, e.g. Pascal 'The eternal silence of these infinite spaces frightens me'.[6]

Robert Frost put his finger on a related issue in his *Desert Places:*

> *They cannot scare me with their empty spaces*
> *Between stars – on stars where no human race*
> *is.*
> *I have it in me so much nearer home*
> *To scare myself with my own desert places.*

---

6 Blaise Pascal, Pensées, number 206

Is there life elsewhere in the Universe?

If we believe Eddington's multiplication table, then there are about ten thousand million, million, million stars in the Universe. We need a sun to provide us with light and warmth – it does not seem possible for life to survive without a sun. Our sun is not special and it seems many stars have planets, so there are probably many places where life could arise. My impression is that life scientists are not yet totally clear how life arose on Earth, but feel that it is not that exceptional; the currently favoured environment for it to start seems to be in hot water springs or vents. Given the size of the Universe I am inclined to believe that there is (or has been, or will be) intelligent life somewhere else in it. We may be lucky and find there is life on a planet not too far from here, but more probably 'they' will be much further away; given the huge distances and the consequent large light-travel times making contact with 'them' will be difficult. Those who believe we humans are a special creation will find it hard to accept that there is intelligent life elsewhere. If we believe in the Incarnation, do we believe there was an Incarnation there too, or are we special in that respect? Did they need a Saviour? Or does God only care about us?

Future of life on Earth

There is rightly considerable concern about the way humankind is altering the environment on this planet, with a risk that we will make the planet uninhabitable. I want to acknowledge this concern but not dwell on it, turning instead to areas where I have particular expertise and considering the long-term future of the Earth assuming we avoid these environmental consequences. However, it is not any more cheerful, just longer drawn out!

We know that in the past the Earth has been hit by large asteroids. There was a major hit about 65 million years ago which many scientists (but not all) believe caused the mass extinction of many species, most famously the dinosaurs. Clearly the part of the Earth where a big asteroid lands is seriously affected. The rest of the world is also affected because a lot of dust is put into the atmosphere, which cuts out sunlight and causes failure of harvests across a much larger area. There is now a large programme to search for potentially hazardous incoming asteroids; at any one time about a thousand objects are being monitored. They are objects believed to be more than 200 metres in diameter and with the possibility of passing closer to the Earth than 20 times the Moon's distance. The monitoring is to determine better the orbit of each of these objects; if the monitoring reveals that they actually fall outside these limits then they are no longer watched. We believe that we should get at least several years' warning of a serious impact and that given this sort of notice we should be able to put into action ways of deflecting the incoming asteroid and preventing it colliding with Earth.

There are other astronomical phenomena which will cause the end of the Earth (or at least the end of life on the Earth). The first of these astronomical phenomena occurs about one billion years from now. As the Sun moves through its 'hydrogen-burning' phase its temperature gradually rises, increasing the heating of the Earth. In about a billion years the temperature will be high enough to boil the oceans and at that point we (if we still exist) will either have to retreat underground or go find another planet (preferably uninhabited) to live on.

The next major astronomical event we need to look out for occurs about three billion years from now when it seems that the Andromeda Galaxy (M31) will collide with the Milky Way. As explained earlier, the chances of a direct hit are extremely small, given how very empty is a galaxy, but tidal effects due to gravity could mean that the Solar System gets flung out to the outer reaches of the galaxy. As long as we stay with the Sun that would not be fatal, but it would remove our option of migrating to another planet in another solar system when or if life here became too hot.

The third major astronomical hazard comes about five billion years from now when our sun runs out of hydrogen in its core and swells to become a red giant star. It will swell about a hundred-fold, which means it will engulf the planets Mercury and Venus. It is not clear whether it will engulf Earth or just come uncomfortably close and make the Earth a cinder. Either way, it is not good for life on Earth.

So it looks likely that one way or another the life of humankind on planet Earth will be exterminated. It may be possible to organise a mass migration (a modern Noah's Ark) by spaceship to another Earth-like planet orbiting another sun-like star, but it will be a long journey with generations spending the whole of their lives on the spaceship and those reaching the new Earth never having known the old Earth.

We have long known that on Earth species can become extinct, and that we are one such species. I suspect we have always assumed that with our intelligence we were in some superior category to the other species and could prevent our own extinction. What astronomy is showing us is that we cannot control nature to the extent we assumed, and in particular we cannot control the evolution of the Sun or the movement of a Galaxy. We are forced to a more careful consideration of the continuation of our species and a recognition that our superior intelligence may not save us in the end.

Future of life elsewhere in the Universe

Could we survive by moving to another planet around another star? Yes, until that star reached the end of its life, and then we could move to another and so on. But the long-term future of the Universe is black and bleak. As the stars shine they use up hydrogen; the amount of hydrogen in the Universe is decreasing. There will come a time when the cycle of star birth, star life, star death and yet more star birth ceases because of lack of hydrogen in the Universe; the old stars will go out and no new stars will light. Galaxies will go black and all life in the Universe will die, will be exterminated; no life will be possible.

We live in a physical universe that is cold, dark, largely empty (and getting colder, darker and emptier); that has no centre or focus; that does not need us, indeed is hostile to us; that seems amoral, purposeless and meaningless. We seem to live in a 'once and only' or 'one-shot' universe. We know that our individual lives are fleeting; maybe the Universe is fleeting too. We are living with the reality that nothing lasts; we need to learn to love anyway.

The meaning of hope

How can we have hope in the face of such predictions? In part I believe it depends on what we mean by hope. We tend to believe that hope is about happy endings, about things coming out OK in the end, and if that is what we believe we are in trouble here!

There is an alternative understanding of what hope means. It is one that says hope is less about the future and more about the now; it is an attitude, stubborn and persistent, consistently doing what feels to be right and not giving up, even when things are dark. It is about identifying things that are good, and putting effort into them; it's about finding meaning in all forms of existence. It's about believing that through such actions we may bring something to fulfilment.

Is this what incarnation means today?

The observant will note that in adopting this definition of hope I am retreating from the long-term, overview picture and focussing on the short-term and relatively local. This seems to be the best I can do at the moment.

The origin of the Universe

We saw earlier that the Universe very probably began from an extremely small volume and expanded out from that. Scientists cannot say where that very small volume came from, or how the laws of physics that have governed its subsequent evolution were established. There are of course plenty of suggestions and theories because we do not like not knowing! Not knowing this is a bit like lacking the first few pages of a book; perhaps people adopted at a young age similarly feel they lack information about their origins.

Religious people would love me to say that God was responsible; that the small volume containing everything was put there by God and that God laid down the laws of physics and so determined the evolution of the Universe. In other words, to say that God filled that gap that the scientists cannot explain. I am reluctant to do this – it reminds me too much of a 'God of the Gaps' theology.

The God of the Gaps theology arose from a time when the power of science was beginning to be recognised but before scientific processes were well understood or were complete. The scientists of the time could explain in part how something came about, but there were gaps in their understanding. Being pious people they attributed the bits they could not explain to God's action. Then scientific knowledge increased and gradually the gaps in our understanding closed. As a consequence God was no longer needed as part of the explanation. So God was out of a job and the image of God suffered as a consequence.

It may turn out to be wrong to say that we can never understand how the early Universe came to be, but at the moment it does seem that we can never know that. Nevertheless, given our experience in previous generations in asserting God did the things we do not understand, I prefer a more robust theology and wish to refrain from saying God started the Universe. I refuse to assume that and suspect the Universe created itself without the intervention of a God.

My theology

Recognising that there was not going to be any proof of the existence of God, I decided many years ago to adopt as a 'working hypothesis' the assumption that there was a God, a God that I will describe below, and to see how I got on with this picture of God. Perhaps evidence would accumulate that would lead me to decide that the hypothesis was wrong, that there was no God, or that God was very different from what I had imagined. Or perhaps evidence would accumulate that made it unquestionably clear that there was a God, maybe even evidence that God was much as I had envisaged. I have not (yet) felt the need to abandon that hypothesis, the roof has not fallen in, and I still have a sense of the numinous! While my understanding of some dimensions of the hypothesis has developed markedly I have not felt the need to change it much. On the other hand I have not had resounding confirmation that it is the right theology – but it would have been very startling if that had happened! It is a picture that works for me – I cannot claim more than that. It may be of interest to others so I share it here.

Another factor in developing my current image of God has come through struggling with questions around suffering: how there can be suffering if God is both loving and all-powerful; and what is the ministry of those of us who have disabilities or wounds that will never heal or will take a very long time to heal? I find it impossible to believe that God can be both loving and omnipotent – too many people are too badly hurt for that to be a tenable combination. The traditional 'explanations' for suffering offered by the Christian church I find unconvincing, and in some instances immoral.

So I looked to see what would be the effect of relinquishing one of the two attributes. I found I had not the courage to do away with the image of a loving God, but I could contemplate a God who was not all-powerful. Maybe God chooses not to use God's power or maybe God is unable to prevent hurt and suffering, I do not know which. So my hypothesis includes a loving God who is not in control of the world.[7]

So I do believe in a God, I believe there is something more to life than physical existence – that there is an inner life. However, I have changed God's job description. I do not believe in a God who was the prime creator – the initiator of our physical universe; the physical universe seems to me to be purposeless. I envisage a loving, caring, supportive, empowering God, a God who works through people (as St Teresa of Avila said, 'He has no hands but ours'); a God of inspiration. This God has not flung thunderbolts at me (which is not to say that life has been entirely

---

7 There is a fuller account in my 1989 Britain Yearly Meeting Swarthmore Lecture 'Broken for Life'. Quaker Books, Friends House, London. Reprinted 2003.

easy) and Meeting for Worship continues to be an important part of my life and the place where I most often meet God.

If God did not create the Universe then God is not responsible for the remarkable natural world that surrounds us, the beautiful scenery, the magnificent sunsets. Whilst these can be very moving and turn us towards God, they do not prove that there is a God. Also if God is not in control of the world then it is not logical to pray that God intervenes and makes the weather better, or makes us pass that exam. Furthermore if God is not in control of the world then God cannot be blamed when things that go badly, nor take the credit when things go well!

And finally, some process points to note. My astronomy and my Quakerism have grown up together and are comfortable bedfellows. But note which bedfellow has done the accommodating! My scientific understanding emerges unscathed by contact with Quakerism. My Quaker bedfellow has bent to fit in with what I have learnt as an astronomer. I have wondered if this is because I am light on Quaker theology in this area, or indeed whether Quaker theology is light in this area. Whilst I have talked with scientists about science and the scientific method, there has not been much place to talk with Quaker theologians on these sorts of topic.

Secondly, readers will have already noticed that I do not feel I have to buy a package of religious beliefs – I can make up my own package, and provided I remain open to revising that package in the light of fresh experience or knowledge, that is OK.

6. This I also know

So far the material presented here has been intellectual and rational – head rather than heart. For a long time it troubled me that I did not seem to be able to integrate into that material what my heart was telling me, what I was feeling in Meeting for Worship, what I was learning through encounters with God. This problem may well be shared by anyone who is both an academic and a mystic. I have recently come to accept that in religion (as indeed in life) there are other ways of knowing – that there are other, different 'languages', and they all have validity.

I have long had a sense of the numinous, and suspect that in other societies I might be labelled a mystic. Encounter with God, communion, has always been very important to me, and it mostly, but not always, happens in Meeting for Worship. Remarkably I find that in a good Meeting for Worship science and religion questions, like the ones I have been struggling with here, float away and become unimportant and irrelevant as I settle into worship.

Here I want to try to articulate and explore what we know about God from other ways. These other ways seem to me to be largely intuitive – we sense things. It is an a-rational way of working, that is, not based on logic or reason. (Note the distinction between a-rational and ir-rational which means illogical or not reasonable). In this area we are all quite idiosyncratic and may prefer different vocabularies. I hope readers will be able to hear what is behind the words I use, to hear where the words come from. We also all have different experiences and whilst what I say will be recognised immediately by some readers, others may feel they and I live on different planets! There is room for all of us, and there is no one right form of words.

I 'know' there is a God, a living, loving God who works through people, prompting, nudging. A God of inspiration, of creativity; a God we can sense in the silence of a gathered Quaker meeting. One who holds a mirror up to us so that we can see our behaviour, keep our standards. One before whom masks, poses and postures drop away; one who knows us as perhaps only our parents knew us; there we are most truly ourselves.

I know that in a good Meeting for Worship what is required of me is that I am present before God, that I am silent and still and let go of things that are not at that moment relevant. I have not words to worship with (sometimes I find myself using the word 'creator', but know it is not meant in any literal sense!); I move beyond words.

So close is the sense of communion that breathing becomes prayer. I encounter a God who supports us, cares for us, grieves with us, empowers us and acts through us in the world, but particularly at such moments calms, heals, holds and sends us out again a little more sensitive, a little wiser, to make a better world.

I am aware that I have been several times prompted to minister in a Meeting for Worship, or to speak on a particular topic, without understanding why, but follow that leading and do so, subsequently to discover I was speaking to a need unknown to me. Over time I have learnt to pay attention to such promptings, but suspect I still fail to recognise some.

In my own Meeting I try to be aware of where the Meeting for Worship has got to and what it needs at that point. There are times when I have to draw strength from the Meeting to minister. Of course Meeting is not always like that! In my case being too busy may be the greatest inhibitor, or being too tired through being too busy.

There is a suggestion that religion is a human construct, that it is all in the brain, that neuro-science will, in a few years, explain it all. Neuro-science is certainly riding high at the moment, has plenty of confidence and is making all sorts of claims. I doubt if they can all be true, but we will have to wait and see which are and which are not! Sometimes I have had promptings to speak which spoke to needs that I did not know existed, things that even my subconscious could not have been aware of, so I am not sure that religion is just a human construct. On balance I am inclined to believe in an external God.

God and Nature

While I am suspicious of statements like 'That is a beautiful sunset – it just proves there must be a God', nevertheless I do appreciate beautiful sunsets! A beautiful sunset, beautiful scenery, beautiful music or poetry does not prove the existence of God but can serve as pointers to prayer or worship of God. Such experiences can bring us to the point where prayer or communion begins, to what in Celtic circles is called a 'thin place', where other worlds are very close.

For some of us nature is a window. I had such an experience recently on a walking holiday in the Swiss Alps. It was towards the end of the holiday when the group I was walking with was comfortable with itself. We had paused for a rest when someone remarked how very quiet it was and we all fell silent and kept still to hear the quiet. It was utterly still, and standing there with that group I felt a door opening to another place; the stillness and the beautiful surroundings led to a sense of reverence and a (silent) prayer of gratitude and joy came spontaneously. It was like in a gathered Quaker Meeting for Worship; I was alive there on that mountainside but elsewhere also, fully in this world but aware of another also. I was touching the hem of transcendence, in a moment of eternity.

Our spiritual nourishment

One of the issues for unprogrammed Friends, I judge, is where we get our spiritual 'nourishment'. Several decades ago I started noting quotes that I liked in a little book; it has become a rich collection of sayings, bits of psalms, prayers, poetry, gathered over a lifetime. I have been lucky enough to find kindred spirits in almost every meeting I have belonged to, and that has encouraged and sustained me. I have also been lucky enough to do quite a lot of ecumenical work for Friends and more recently to serve the world body of Friends, the Friends World Committee for Consultation.

I now know from ecumenical work that people of other denominations can through their faith and practice show me God, particularly if I can suspend the rational. I know there are revealing insights in other faiths' beliefs and practices. I know through Friends World Committee work that people from different flavours of Quakerism, with different beliefs about the Bible and different ways of practising their Quakerism can, especially through their worship, help me worship God and be refreshed.

Jesus Christ has not had much mention! I have been considering God rather than Christ because I feel I need to be clear on the God-role first before thinking about Christ. However my theology keeps bumping into traditional Christian beliefs, which is uncomfortable. I recognise that the life of Jesus gives us a very high standard to live up to. I know the Bible as well as many British Friends and I value it for the wisdom in it, but judge it is not to be read as a scientific document.

I enjoy (and enjoy leading) Bible study which is loosely based on Jewish Midrash. Midrash is an attempt to fill in many of the gaps in a Bible story*. Although no Jew would recognise what I do as proper Midrash, I have found that working with a creative group of Friends can be moving, thought-provoking, full of insights, and even on occasion hilarious.

[* For further information about Midrash see en. wikipedia.org/wiki/Midrash.]

Do we need myths? In particular, do we need myths for religion, explaining how the world and humankind came to be? I am very conscious that this lecture has destroyed myth without providing any alternative. Or perhaps it is the over-literal interpretation of myth that has been destroyed. Where and how do we get myths appropriate for the contemporary age? Or is that a non-starter – are myths totally incompatible with a scientific and technical culture? I have no answers to these questions and see them as pointing to an area for future work for all of us.

We saw in Chapter 2 how professional scientists spend a lot of time doubting and how certainty (and over-confidence) can de-rail the scientific method. Some consider doubt a weakness, but for me it is far healthier than certainty, although it does need to be seen as something open and flexible, not disabling. As has often been said, certainty rather than doubt is the opposite of faith.

I finish with a favourite quotation:

Be patient towards all that is unsolved in your heart ... do not now seek the answers which cannot be given because you would not be able to live them ... live the questions now[8] .

---

8 Rainer Maria Rilke (1903) Letters to a Young Poet

Appendix

Further reading in astronomy and cosmology

Bryson, Bill (2004) *A Short History of Nearly Everything.* Black Swan.

Chown, Marcus and Schilling, Govert (2011). *Tweeting the Universe.* Faber and Faber.

Greene, Brian (2011) *The Hidden Reality.* Allen Lane.

Panek, Richard (2011) *The 4% Universe.* Oneworld Publications.

Radford, Tim (2011) *The Address Book.* Fourth Estate.

Rees, Martin (2001) *Just Six Numbers; the Deep Forces that Shape the Universe.* Orion Books.

The World Wide Web is also a rich source of information, although the standard of reliability is variable. *Wikipedia* is normally reliable, as are academic web sites and those of professional bodies.

THE JAMES BACKHOUSE LECTURES

1994 *As the Mirror Burns: Making a Film about Vietnam,* Di Bretherton

1995 *Emerging Currents in the Asia-Pacific,* DK Anderson & BB Bird

1996 *Our Children, Our Partners – a New Vision for Social Action in the 21st Century,* Elise Boulding

1997 *Learning of One Another: The Quaker Encounter with Other Cultures and Religions,* Richard G Meredith

1998 *Embraced by Other Selves: Enriching Personal Nature through Group Interaction,* Charles Stevenson

1999 *Myths and Stories, Truths and Lies,* Norman Talbot

2000 *To Learn a New Song: A Contribution to Real Reconciliation with the Earth and its Peoples,* Susannah Kay Brindle

2001 *Reconciling Opposites: Reflections on Peacemaking in South Africa,* Hendrik W van der Merwe

2002 *To Do Justly, and to Love Mercy: Learning from Quaker Service*, Mark Deasey

2003 *Respecting the Rights of Children and Young People: A New Perspective on Quaker Faith and Practice*, Helen Bayes

2004 *Growing Fruitful Friendship: A Garden Walk*, Ute Caspers

2005 *Peace is a Struggle*, David Johnson

2006 *One Heart and a Wrong Spirit: The Religious Society of Friends and Colonial Racism*, Polly O Walker

2007 *Support for Our True Selves: Nurturing the Space Where Leadings Flow*, Jenny Spinks

2008 *Faith, Hope and Doubt in Times of Uncertainty: Combining the Realms of Scientific and Spiritual Inquiry*, George Ellis

2009 *The Quaking Meeting: Transforming Our Selves, Our Meetings and the More-than-human World*, Helen Gould

2010 *Finding our voice: Our truth, community and journey as Australian Young Friends*, Australian Young Friends

2011 *A demanding and uncertain adventure: Exploration of a concern for Earth restoration and how we must live to pass on to our children,* Rosemary Morrow

2012 *From the inside out: Observations on Quaker work at the United Nations,* David Atwood

Backhouse Lectures, as well as other Australia Yearly Meeting publications, are available from Friends Book Sales, sales@quakers.org.au and sales@ipoz.bi z.

Back Cover Material

Can a scientist also be religious? How, and with what limitations? This lecture describes astronomers' current understanding of the Universe we live in and shows how the lecturer combines her Quakerism and her science.

Made in the USA
San Bernardino, CA
08 March 2018